GW01057437

EXPERIMENTAL
PLACEMENT

Indigo Dreams Publishing

D565656 1 893277

First Edition: Breakfast Under a Yellow-bellied Sun
First published in Great Britain in 2019 by:
Indigo Dreams Publishing Ltd
24 Forest Houses
Halwill
Beaworthy
EX21 5UU
www.indigodreams.co.uk

Graham Burchell has asserted his right under the Copyright, Designs and Patents Act 1988 to be identified as the author of this work.

ISBN 978-1-912876-02-0

British Library Cataloguing in Publication Data. A CIP record for this book can be obtained from the British Library.

Designed and typeset in Palatino Linotype by Indigo Dreams.
Cover design by Ronnie Goodyer at Indigo Dreams

Printed and bound in Great Britain by: 4edge Ltd
www.4edge.co.uk

Papers used by Indigo Dreams are recyclable products made from wood grown in sustainable forests following the guidance of the Forest Stewardship Council.

For Linda and David Cox

Acknowledgements

Acknowledgements are due to the following in which some of these poems (or versions of them) first appeared:
I Lay my Head, Masked Lapwing and Breakfast Under a Yellow-bellied sun – *Poetry Saltzburg*, Winter 2017/18
She's The Pied Piper – *The Broadsheet*, 2016
Pinjarra and Me – *The Foxglove Journal*, August 2017
Blue Lake – the anthology, *Watermarks: New Writing by Lido Lovers and Wild Swimmers*
I Talk to Cormorants – Zoomorphic marine wildlife-themed anthology, *Driftfish*
Mountain Ashes and Nightmare with Small Perching Birds – *The Dawntreader*.

Also by Graham Burchell:

Vermeer's Corner (2008), Foothills Publishing (New York)
The Chongololo Club (2012), Pindrop Press
Cottage Pi (2015), SPM Publications
Kate (2015), Indigo Dreams Publishing Ltd

CONTENTS

Chelyabinsk

Chelyabinskans have seven words for pine scents I've decided,
but only one for bodies of water.
Nobody, not even the ruler has ever seen the sea.

Chelyabinsk, until today I'd never heard of you,
but the map on the screen on the back of the seat in front of me
suggests that you exist, that you are near.

Chelyabinskans, I think of you shivering within your city walls,
flooding out when the air is right to gather pine straw and fungi,
to harvest resins for burning as offerings in minareted

Chelyabinsk churches to appease the silver messengers
that sometimes pass above, spy, paint the sky with a white tail
on their way to report to an amber-perfumed god.

Karaganda

Karagandans have seven words for coal I've decided,
but only one for bodies of water.

Until today, I'd never heard of it, or its citizens
in their boiler suits and head scarves, faces like putty
in winter, scorched roses in summer.

It must be a rail town, with sidings, iron sheds, waste land
with summer weeds and abandonment.

Karagandans will have small eyes.
There's surely nothing to view beyond the coming and going
of half mile trains to take away its black gold.

And there'll be no churches or residue of prayer.
No one will feel that need or see the point of mumbling at the
sky.

That's where I am, waving in my mind
to your name on a map on a screen
in a plane.

I Lay my Head...

on a bed where so many have lain before,
my eyes considering a flat ceiling
for the first time in a brace of displaced days.

I shut them. It's ten in the morning here.
I try to sleep, roll to the left, think about gravity,
how it sticks me to the mattress in this student cell,
abused for generations in a college that sits
so gently in its green.

I ponder all the homesickness festered here,
all the essays contrived, the alcohol, vomit,
tears spilled, love made on this single bed...

...my eyes jolt open. I'd become foetal, slept,
woke to two tiny cockroaches exploring
the far border of my pillow.

At the edge of my dream I'd heard a bird let go
its exotic riff, its assemblage of hoots and gulps.
It repeats them, repeats, pulls me up, floats me
to the window because, I'm in Sydney
and I need to know.

She's the Pied Piper...

of Sydney in a pale green t-shirt: the pipe, her voice,
velvet over an afternoon engine of traffic.
Stay with the T-shirt, she calls, and hypnotised
a swarm of the inquisitive follow.

I am under that trance. My feet find new flagstones,
test unfamiliar tarmac, become part of a weave
that stops only when the piper stops
to play familiar refrains before expected icons,

with words manipulated, slanted, pitched
like names with letters pulled out, shoed in
switched, clipped, attached to dates that allude
to a sidestepped history.

Here's a statue of Victoria fly-tipped from Dublin.
Now we're in Hyde Park, note the ibises and this,
our cenotaph, our quirky alley with dangling
birdcages and our opera house,

shaped like giant moon shells bunched in the shade
of that bridge. She pipes us to where it curves
like an eyebrow, a steel rainbow.
This is where our walkabout ends, she says.

Pinjarra and Me

Pinjarra, the saltwater crocodile at Melbourne Sea-Life Aquarium

We came into the world in the same year
you
chased out of a shell
and into the muddle of mud and mangrove

me
snipped slapped weighed and wrapped

for you
it was crocodile breath the press of a mother's teeth
and the first flush of river

for me
it was the touch of fabrics voices the breath
of last adult meals and afternoon light

perhaps we were born on the same day
same moment to be axis points on a globe

you
with your long leathered face
silent hunger and cold blood in brackish water

me
with my green bones and jellyfish flesh turning
towards cathedral bells beyond the walls of the room

we are each sixty five years old separated by glass
along the way we've made mistakes

you
for being in the wrong place after a flood
for becoming stranded on a Queensland farm

me
how long have you got

now look at us

Bush Turkey

A warning. *Achtung!* Crocodiles - keep away
from the water's edge. I was reading that
when I heard, then glimpsed a long toothless face,
its tail a paddle, not armour and swipe, but a fiddle of feathers.

It back-kicked in a pile of leaves
like Gollum aching to find the lost ring.
The eye that scoured was moon shadow over butter sun;
an orb within a red flame.

That summer, it wore a yellow scarf, black coat and shorts.
It didn't care – wasn't bothered by my being there,
or that it looked brash and gaunt with its bulbous beak
in a head full of folds, holes and remnant hair.

Blue Lake

Blue Lake, Mount Gambier, South Australia

An expletive burst from me like a sneeze
when it was first glimpsed between trees,

and being three or four times as intense as the sky,
a monomictic crater's eye in extinct volcanic maar,

I announced that no body of water should take
colour so far, not even when seventy metres deep.

I considered its small fish, lovers of blue perhaps,
that evolved to wear it, body, fins, tail, eyes.

They'll not be visible to each other of their kind
until autumn starts to fade, and the lake dies

to a winter grey, a time of recognition,
of being in season, of falling for
an opposite's cobalt hue.

Satin Bower Bird

Are you spying with your wary violet eye,
from a limb of red cedar?

Are you picking over bins for something blue?
Are you snatching spilled sultanas
from a picnic table before bush turkeys do?

I see your door is open.
I peek between green blade walls to a carpet
of leaf litter bejewelled with drinking straws,
sweet wrappers and lots and lots of bottle tops – all blue.

It's a splendid layout, the half-built bower,
the way you've left a centrepiece of weathered stone.
I love the subtle shades of the chosen colour.

But really, is this how it has to look
to have her fall for you?

Rainforest Love Story

Pandorea pandorana (Wonga vine) I heard
how you played a shy sapling to death,
how you spiralled ambition
with just a hint of lust without love
so that he wept withered
and you became a needy
empty helix

you searched for another
a black booyong felt your caress
warmed but later wanted you off
too clingy self-absorbed
so you shamelessly looped over
to his mate scrub bloodwood
taken in at first a lover of closeness
but he wouldn't amount to much

and you reached for a tall redhead
a red carabeen who was loaded
what you were hankering for
he would show you the canopy a sky
full of light where you'd flower
he was happy to let you
suck him dry

Mountain Ashes

We call ours Rowan,
a magic lady-like hermaphrodite with nickelled bark,
fid na ndruad, a wizard's tree, brazen in churchyards
with dangling earrings of bloody berries, and planted
near houses to bring luck, ward off.

One should never be felled, *they* said,
but its wood was snipped to make spoons
                 to stir milk
                   to stop it curdling.

Its wood was snipped to make pocket charms,
                 to shun rheumatics,
                 to produce rods for divining.

Australia, your mountain ashes, your *Eucalyptus regnans*,
leprous giants, world's tallest flowering plants, floating
on deep loam in Victorian rain forest are magic too.

One seed grain becomes an arboreal body builder,
or a chorister with autumn flowers in its hair,
white like its voice.

Or it becomes a memorial, stretching or scabbing
over words and love codes carved into its ankle,
and as far up its shin as desecraters can carve
their names or their transient love:

Mike Joey Chaz Arni Mia XXY T+P
heart   heart   heart

Three Sisters

From a story based on the three weathered rock stacks in the Blue Mountains,
New South Wales

Meehni

lost her head.
She feels for her sister's hand.
Even time cannot grasp how slowly she reaches,
but within, she recalls the moil of scents
in the valley, animal and eucalyptic.
She climbed because she was told
that from up high she may find love,
even though she had no head for heights,
and on that ridge with the mountains rippled
under its blue gauze, she was petrified.

Wimlah

still has her hair tied in a top knot.
Weathering has not loosened it, nor scoured her beauty.
She'll be a centre of attention for ever, with her eyes-down
look of longing, and a sense of anxiety braced
at the corners of her mouth.
She misses her reflection in a pool of the river,
misses smiling, taunting the Nepean boys -
forbidden love.

Gunnedoo

the eldest, misunderstood, sensitive,
tresses of scribbly gum left loose behind her shoulders,
unbrushed. She doesn't mind.
To have them oiling her bare skin is enough.
It reminds her of touch, fingers she had
to strum the saw tooth leaves of banksias

and their candle brush flowers.
She'd been about to say something profound,
but never quite found the words.

Masked Lapwing
Vanellus miles novaehollandiae

Some other bird's great uncle in a black hat,
a professor, a judge, a Wesleyan minister,
alone on grassy wasteland reflecting
on an academic past.

He wears a favourite lightweight light brown jacket
on his shoulders over a cricket jumper.
Those liver-red trousers he's had since the eighties
do not disguise his pencil legs.

He's lived with the jibes. He's oblivious,
and when they call him masked lapwing,
he alone knows it's not a mask at all,
but egg on his face for a foolish moment
never to be retold.

Cape Otway Road

with forks in white trees,
oiled and warmed by the grey cheeks
of koala bears.

I Talk to Cormorants...

time-wasting on a rock defecated white;
pied cormorants that I call mates.

I admire their plumage,
the fit of dark on top of light.

I tell them, and they have no answers,
no taste for words,

though if mine brought fish of course...

But long yellow beaks hold still
above the water's lift and slap.

I ask if I should go. I tell them it was nice
talking to them. I mean it.

One nods. One starts to preen.
Three others watch their wings dry.

On an Island at Night Waiting for Fairies

Wary in daylight, they're at sea,
what's left of them - twenty six this year.
A few remember fifteen hundred, more,
coming ashore on this their Granite Island
before the long causeway was built,
to give a way for cats, for pet diseases.

White light hurts them too, too bright
for salty little eyes, so it's a red torch beam,
a red oval, that scans for a muted Tinkerbell
while pressed against railings, sheltered
from ocean bluster.
                    I don't believe in fairies
until one is there, nailed, and my breath
is stilled.
              Wings twitch for balance.
It falters, waddles with a pirate's gait,
sea legs on land, first fairy,
tiniest of penguin kind.

According to yearly surveys, the colony of Fairy Penguins on Granite Island,
Victor Harbor, South Australia, has crashed from 1548 in 2001 to just 26 last
year (2015).

Passing Through Port Noarlunga

A cycle event.
They pass in sudden murders, squawking,
sounding more avian than birds;
tyre growl overlaid with excitement.

A couple, laggers,
enjoy the ride, and when he twists
shouts back to her, *what are ya fuckin doing?*
I can tell that it's rhetorical, imbued with love.

A Town Called Quorn

I pull into a quad with motel rooms down
each long side, and look for the reception.
It's locked but has a note pinned to the door to
inform the reader of the receptionist's profound
apology for her absence.

I feel myself cooking because as I read these words,
the temperature is the wrong side of forty.
I learn as I bake that the keys are in the doors,
so I check each one with its dangling label.

I can hardly hear myself for the din
made by squawking galahs in a tree in the far corner.
Each label is for someone in the Groovy Grape party –
nothing for me.

It's too hot to linger, so I drive
to find some kangaroos in a nearby reserve
before returning, hoping the receptionist
has found her way back to the office
because it's four o'clock in the afternoon.

However, it occurs to me that I haven't seen anyone.
I expect to drive over drifting tumbleweed
as I head up the main street, turn off into a side road
and up the driveway to the motel for a second time.

The reception is still shut and the note untouched.
It occurs to me that the receptionist isn't going
to appear, so I may have to use my mobile phone.
I don't want to. They shouldn't assume that I have one
with or without a charged battery,

but considering the alternative and how far it is
to find anywhere else to stay, I rummage
through my rucksack, then heave a suitcase
from the boot to the floor,

and on finally finding the damned thing
with rolled up socks in a shoe, I return to the note,
find a number, realise I have about a minute
of talk time left.

I dial, hear a voice telling me that I'm in Australia
(as if I didn't know already), and that I would be
charged at a different rate. I swear at the voice
before hanging up to tap out the number again,

to hear another voice, female, and I shout at her
because she is too calm. Doesn't she know how hot it is?
She tells me too calmly that there is a key box
outside my room, room eleven.

I demand the code and explain that my phone
is about to die. I'm about to die. She says
try one two three four, which I do and a flap flies open
to reveal a golden key. I beg her to stay on the line
while I try it in the door. It clicks open.

I let her know with a sudden shunt of good humour,
but the phone has expired, is dead, *muerte*,
and all I hear is squawking galahs in a tree
in the far corner and a fly that wants to dance
all over my face.

Breakfast Under a Yellow-bellied Sun
for Yvonne

The 'Skin So Soft' product that you promised
would ward off biting insects, works.
My legs are like satin, the texture of some exotic fruits
found in containers in the fridge; those to be taken
with tea and toast on the veranda,
where sunlight is fragile, ephemeral like life.
Between spoonfuls of soursop and mamey sapote,
there's a shock of soft torrential rain that passes
like a wavering curtain to leave a tap-dance of drips,
before the yellow-bellied sun dares to show itself again,
before a yellow-bellied sunbird is conjured
between the blush pink spathes of a tropical flower,
its thrumming heart kernelled in quilted patches
of indigo, yellow and brown.

Coffee in Cairns

He strikes with a question and exclamation mark.
He thunders. He's a charging bull,
and the assailed, like a small mammal caught in headlights,
has no chance to dodge before the first is on him,
horned, snorting, rifling pockets.

Where's my money?

I with the innocence of morning coffee, cross
from a café on the corner on the same side of the same street,
to a vacant table. Two women, late teens, skirt around me,
walk in the road.

What have you done with my money? Give it to me.

The smaller man's grubby sack is ripped from his shoulders.
Meaty fingers unzip, unflap, plunge and delve.

Give me what you've got. Give me my fucking money.

I sit in the chair furthest from the gutter, open my notebook,
and the smaller man, the wastrel, runt of his litter
tries to bark back.

I haven't got your money.

I peer into a white cup, raise the heat to my face.
There's a yelp. I look up. The bullied, creased with pain,
turns towards me.

I find a pen, lift it to an empty page and take a first sip.
He rushes past, knocks my chair.
The other chases.

Come here motherfucker.

They *exeunt* (stage right) into the next street.
For a moment, all I hear is the high-pitched babble
of flying foxes in the tree on the next corner.
I consider an opening line, sip again and wait for toast.

Lunch with the Kurds

I'm only a hundred miles south of Port Arthur.
That's a line I could sing to Gene Pitney's
signature song as I pull into a rest area without shade,
like so many I have seen, picnic tables, bins,
an oak leaf of shelter and an acre of heat.

I sit in the car, engine thrumming, air-con running.
The closed window is a barrier.
I'm not certain why I've stopped.
Was it fatigue, or more a need for food or water?

A family pick over lunch.
I switch off, regard them, ponder on where I am,
a dot between a metropolis and a town.
I slip closer towards an emptiness they call outback.

I get out to open the boot, see what I have,
and as soon as the door is closed,
before the first fly hits my face, my eyes, I'm beckoned -
no mistake.

A man sat at a picnic table has me on a string,
reels me in. What else can I do, but draw close,
smile, greet, sit when he demands, stumble
in my thinking when he alone tells me to join in,
have lunch with them.

I've no choice. This isn't up for debate,
and when I'm slow to dig in, he starts to pile the plate
put before me. *Help yourself. Take what you want.*
He does all the talking, the animation. The others eat,
talk amongst themselves.

And while I fork lamb that falls from the bone,
he tells me they have moved from Sydney to Adelaide -
much better. He tells me they are Kurdish.
As soon as I saw you, he says, *I told my family,*
I am going to ask that man to share our food.

First Movement

I compose as I beat your bounds Uluru,
water slapping in bottles between my shoulder blades,
a fly net perfumed with repellent under my hat.
I compose in double time, more for deference
than boot steps, with a thin orchestral cast
and one cello transcendent.
I begin where the rock has an eye,
one high in the scoured folds of a face
that looks out over trees gathered like pilgrims.
They wait there with a great thirst,
with unseen small birds in their heads.

The opening motif will be four notes,
an arc of measured intervals, repeated, inverted,
becoming skittish like the skip-dash of a lizard
tasting a rush of open space.
I wander into sacred parts and barely dare
to snatch a sideways glance,
but those four notes will not leave me -
dum dum di dooh, dum dum di dooh.
The *dooh* pulled taut, bowed sorrowfully,
as if issued from a pressure point
far across the monolith's spine.

This will be a sadness fit for mimicry,
for brass, French horns for a wail,
for envy of a little willie wagtail
(half corvid, half angel), with grey legs
perched either side of a hairline fissure.
The envy will not be of its syncopated bird speak
somewhere between whistle-squeak and crow,
but of its moves, the dip and wag,
the *dum dum di dooh,* like wind that comes here rarely,
that has to pilot a way over or around
this monumental interruption.

Nightmare with Small Perching Birds

Snouts of winged shrews harden into nibs, seed crackers,
heads of tiny pliers, straight and down-curved,
and many birds (for that's what they become in a breath),
stop to hover before my eyes, theirs no longer black beads,
but meaner, without inhibition, while others, unseen
or half seen, parley in repeated motifs or trills.

Whether high-pitched or higher, all I hear is, *go, go back,*
so my heart beats faster, and I fret about anisodactyl feet,
those sharper than hawthorn that could snag in my hair,
scratch, draw blood from my scalp, from the curve of an ear.
They're ganging, but I see no more than flits, whispers
winged into fully clothed trees

where I look so hard and hear so well, but cannot see them,
commanded by ravens with black-studded white eyes
and stares as dispassionate as the regard of crocodiles.

They in turn answer to the spell of *Yulanya,* offspring
of *Tjinderi-tjinderiba.* I saw one, proud as a prince
with bleached eyebrows, white shirt, black tails
and a stockinged leg either side of a pencil thick rock fissure.
Don't come back tomorrow, it insisted, but here I am,
menaced by both the brazen and the barely seen.

Together, they create a sound wall, a dreadful orchestra
that plays until I'm jumped awake to the spin and shudder
of a ceiling fan, by a threat, the awful possibility
that at the crest of their wild fortissimo, they will hurl
their instruments with deadly aim: piccolos, dented brass,
sopranino recorders and rosin-dusted bows.

Tjinderi-tjinderiba: Willy-wagtail woman from Aboriginal dreamtime stories
connected with Uluru Yulanya: the children of Tjinderi-tjinderiba

Passing Through Wonglepong

I'm not driving,
and I'm totally inured to the flick past of fields,
eucalyptus, occasional signs bearing silhouettes of animals,
or old aboriginal words finding a small home.

Place names that slipped from some other dimension,
that pulled apart those you know and slotted in
woggle or wiggle to become *wongle* fitted to *pong,*
where you think of a bad smell, or a word to go with ping.

So it's difficult to ignore a sign that lets you know
you're entering Wonglepong,
and you shunt into your seatbelt, sit up,
turn to glimpse the plain white back of it.

It's a moment passed.
You mouth it like a fish. Send it as a whisper
round your tongue, for it's child-like ring.

Indigo Dreams Publishing
24 Forest Houses
Halwill
Beaworthy
Devon
EX21 5UU
www.indigodreams.co.uk